Pebble Bilingual Books

Soy bondadosa/ I Am Caring

de/by
Sarah L. Schuette

Traducción/Translation
Martín Luis Guzmán Ferrer, Ph.D.

Capstone Press
Mankato, Minnesota

Pebble Bilingual Books are published by Capstone Press
151 Good Counsel Drive, P.O. Box 669, Mankato, Minnesota 56002
http://www.capstone-press.com

1 2 3 4 5 6 08 07 06 05 04 03

Library of Congress Cataloging-in-Publication Data
Schuette, Sarah L., 1976–
 [I am caring. Spanish & English]
 Soy bondadosa / de Sarah L. Schuette; traducción, Martín Luis Guzmán Ferrer =
I am caring / by Sarah L. Schuette; translation, Martín Luis Guzmán Ferrer.
 p. cm.—(Pebble bilingual books)
 Spanish and English.
 Includes index.
 Summary: Simple text and photographs show different ways of being helpful and
showing that you care.
 ISBN 0-7368-2301-8
 1. Caring—Juvenile literature. [1. Caring. 2. Spanish language materials—
Bilingual.] I. Title: I am caring. II. Title. III. Series: Pebble bilingual books.
BJ1475.S3818 2004
177'.7—dc21   2003004925

Editorial Credits
Mari C. Schuh and Martha E. H. Rustad, editors; Jennifer Schonborn, series designer
 and illustrator; Patrick Dentinger, cover production designer; Nancy White, photo
 stylist; Karen Risch, product planning editor; Eida Del Risco, Spanish copy editor;
 Gail Saunders-Smith, consulting editor; Madonna Murphy, Ph.D., Professor of
 Education, University of St. Francis, Joliet, Illinois, author of *Character Education in
 America's Blue Ribbon Schools*, consultant

Photo Credits
Capstone Press/Gregg Anderson, cover, 10, 12; Gary Sundermeyer, 1, 4, 6, 8, 14, 16,
 18, 20

Pebble Books thanks the Moreno family of Mankato, Minnesota, for modeling in this
book. The author dedicates this book to her aunts, Lois and Ruth Schuldt, of Belle
Plaine, Minnesota.

Table of Contents

Contenido

THANK YOU FOR YOUR DONATIONS
E SORRY, BUT WE CANNOT
PT THE FOLLOWING ITEMS:

Torn or Dirty Clothing
Broken Electrical Items
Chemicals or Paints
Large Appliances
Dehumidifiers
Air Conditioners
Tires

I am a caring person.
I think about the needs
of other people.

Yo soy una persona
bondadosa. Pienso en las
necesidades de los demás.

6

I care about my family.
I give my dad a hug. I
tell him that I love him.

Me importa mi familia.
Le doy un abrazo a mi
papá. Le digo cuánto
lo quiero.

I listen to my sister
when she is sad. I try
to help her feel better.

Escucho a mi hermana
cuando está triste. La
ayudo a sentirse mejor.

I care about my friends.
I visit my friend
when he is hurt.

Me preocupo por mis
amigos. Visito a mi amigo
cuando se enferma.

I tell my friend that she did a good job.

Felicito a mi amiga cuando hace bien las cosas.

I care about animals.

I take care of my pets.

Quiero mucho a los
animales. Yo cuido a
mis animalitos domésticos.

I care about my safety.
I wear my seat belt
in the car.

Me preocupo por mi
seguridad. Uso el cinturón
de seguridad en el auto.

I care about my health.
I eat good food.

Me preocupo por mi salud.
Como alimentos sanos.

I am caring, thoughtful, and kind. I think about myself and others.

Soy bondadosa, atenta y cariñosa. Pienso en mí y en los demás.

Glossary

caring—being concerned about a person or a thing; caring people pay attention to other people's feelings.

kind—to be friendly, helpful, and generous

listen—to pay attention so that you can hear something; caring people pay attention and listen to others.

sad—an unhappy emotion; caring people listen and support others who are sad.

thoughtful—to consider other people's needs and feelings; thoughtful people think carefully before they make a decision; they sometimes put other people's feelings before their own.

visit—to go to see a person or a place; caring people visit other people when they are sick or hurt.

Glosario

bondadoso—preocuparse por una persona o cosa; las personas bondadosas piensan en los sentimientos de los demás.

cariñoso—ser afectuoso, servicial y generoso

escuchar—poner atención para poder oír las cosas; las personas bondadosas prestan atención y escuchan a los demás.

triste—sentimiento de infelicidad; las personas bondadosas escuchan y apoyan a los demás cuando están tristes.

atentar—pensar en los sentimientos y las necesidades de los demás; las personas atentas piensan cuidadosamente antes de tomar una decisión; muchas veces ponen los sentimientos de los demás antes que los propios.

visitar—ir a ver a una persona o a cierto lugar; las personas bondadosas visitan a los demás cuando están enfermos o lastimados.

Index

Índice